Neversink School
and other silly poems

by **Robert Munsch**

illustrated by **Michael Martchenko**

Scholastic Canada Ltd.
Toronto New York London Auckland Sydney
Mexico City New Delhi Hong Kong Buenos Aires

Winter

The great Canadian winter
Is not so very cold.
I once knew a kid who didn't freeze
Until he was ten years old.
And just last year in Ottawa,
When cleaning up the ice,
They found two people still alive
And they said winter was nice.
So don't stay inside when it's snowing,
Don't stay inside when there's ice.
Go out and get frozen like a brick,
And then you'll think winter is nice.

Snow

I'm standing here to catch some snow,
My teacher thinks it's neat.
My hands are full of frostbite;
There's ice cubes on my feet.
I'm also rather worried
About one little thing:
What will this crazy teacher
Think of in the spring!

A Poem of Her Own

Erin had to learn a poem,
A poem to say quite alone,
Yes, a poem all of her own,
To say in front of class.
She looked in books.
She looked in nooks.
She looked and looked
And looked and looked,
Till she ran out of gas.
She finally said,
"I wish I were dead,
'Cause there's no poem inside my head!
The teacher will make me flunk," she said.
"I need a poem to pass."
To make herself feel somewhat better
She went and wrote Bob Munsch a letter,
Hoping he might tell her whether
They could write a poem together.
(It couldn't hurt to ask.)
And he sent her back a poem,
A poem to say quite alone,
Yes, a poem all of her own,
To say in front of class.
Which goes to show,
As you may know,
No matter what stuff life does throw,
It doesn't hurt to ask.

Math Is Deadly

"Mrs. Livesay's
Math is deadly,"
All the children said.
"It makes us want to close our eyes
And jump right into bed."

Alexander

Alexander was a wrestler
And a very fine wrestler was he,
He wrestled his way off to school
And pinned his teacher for three.
The principal was quite upset.
He yelled, "Alex! Stop!"
So Alex wrestled with himself
And still came out on top.

Neversink School

Our school is near the ocean,
It's really rather neat.
Except that crabs come out at lunch
And nibble at our feet;
And yesterday our teacher
Was eaten by a shark,
Because she stayed late to correct
Our homework after dark.
But we like the ocean
And this is our advice:
"Seaside schools are useful
If your teacher isn't nice."

What a Payne!

Mrs. Payne
Had a class
Which—what a pain—
She wouldn't pass!
So Mrs. Payne,
Tough as leather,
Kept them in
Kindergarten
Forever!

Collections

Keira collects
Collections of things,
Pinecones and rocks,
Paper and string,
Ribbons and buttons
And any old thing.

Emlyn constructs
Constructions of things
Pinecones and rocks,
Paper and string,
Ribbons and buttons
That Keira brings.

Partners together
To gather up stuff,
Transforming and adding;
There's never enough.

Piles and piles,
So all can see them.
Goodness gracious!
Our home's a museum!

Terry Lynn

Terry-Lynn in Flin Flon
Collected lots of rocks,
And hid them in her dresser
In a great big cardboard box.
Her mother wished them long gone
And tried to throw them out
But Terry-Lynn from Flin Flon
Did yell and scream and shout.
She's now collecting boulders.
Her mother says it's wrong.
But Terry-Lynn from Flin Flon
Keeps collecting on.

Caleb

Caleb likes Lego
And Lego likes him.
They play well together
With vigour and vim.
They cover the floor
And fill up the house
There's not even room
For a cat or a mouse.
His mother and father
Do sometimes complain
That Caleb likes Lego
And Lego's a pain.
But Caleb is happy
And Caleb is swell;
And if you like Caleb,
Like Lego as well.

Toby

Toby never cleaned his room.
It was so full of dirt
That his mother slipped and fell
And almost got real hurt.
So Toby cleaned for thirty days
And then he cleaned some more,
And when he cleaned for sixty days
He finally saw the floor.

Calvin

Calvin likes bugs
And maybe likes slugs
And maybe worse things
He'll discover.
But I think he's neat
In spite of these feats,
Because he's my little brother.

Katie's Hair

Katie had such long black hair
She couldn't see her mother.
But that was what she had to bear
Or else she'd see her brother.

Twins

My baby sisters
They are two,
And also two they are.
But they don't know
That they are two.
'Cause they can't count
That far.

For Monique

I have a lovely stepbrother
The best I've ever had.
I step on him when things go wrong
And I don't feel so bad.

Oh, Brother!

I have a mean brother,
And also another,
They both are such a pain.
Why doesn't my mother
Sell one or the other
And send them away on a train;
Or put then on loan,
And far from home,
Where I'll never see them again.

Chelsea's Dog Spot

My dad does not like Spot.
He wishes he was not.
He wishes we had got
A 'Not Spot' Spot.
But I like Spot a lot.
I don't wish he was not.
I think it would be sad!
If there's a not,
Let's make it Dad!

Lucy

I have a dog
And her name is Lucy.
She likes kids
When they're nice and juicy.

Jeanette Ran Red

Jeanette ran, red to the sunrise,
In the rainbow shining grass;
Rolling in buttercups
And the sweet smell of morning,
Cold dew soaking her nightgown,
Till the inside smell of coffee and pancakes
Rippled through the Queen Anne's Lace.
So rolling and rollicking,
She shivered coldly through the kitchen door
Dropping dew and buttercups and cut grass
Into the warm food smell of kitchen,
And into her mother's surprised
   "A Springtime Fairy it is,"
Which scooped her up into a very wet
Springtime Hug
Full of worm smell and wet hair.

Jayna's Shadow

My shadow in the morning
Is very very long,
But by the time it's lunchtime
My shadow's almost gone.
It's grown again by dinner.
It's very long and thin.
It gets so big at nighttime.
It lets the stars come in.

Reading

When I was young I liked to read,
And books liked me,
Because together we were more
Than either one could be.

Goodnight

Goodnight, goodnight, my sleepyhead,
And may your sweet dreams find you,
With jellybeans and chocolate bars
While elves and angels mind you.

Page 3
Winter: *I wrote this for my own kids during a cold winter.*

Snow: *A teacher from Missouri sent me a picture of her class trying to catch snowflakes.*

Page 4
A Poem of Her Own: *Erin really did write me a letter asking for a poem. She memorized it and told it at a school contest and she got first prize.*

Page 5
Math Is Deadly: *Mrs. Livesay's class in Texas sent me letters, so I wrote poems for some of them.*

Alexander: *Alexander sent me a picture of himself that said underneath, "I AM A WRESTLER."*

Page 6
Neversink School: *For Navesink School, Atlantic Highlands, New Jersey.*

What a Payne!: *A kindergarten teacher from Mesa, Arizona, wrote me a very nice letter. I just had to use her name in a poem.*

Page 9
Collections: *For Keira and Emlyn, whose mother who told me about their collections.*

Terry-Lynn: *For Terry Lynn Haffich, Flin Flon, Manitoba. "I collect different kinds of neat rocks."*

Page 11
Caleb: *For Caleb Stratton, Ballston Lake, New York. "I invent crazy things with my Legos!"*

Toby: *For Toby, who wrote that his room was always dirty.*

Page 12
Calvin: *Aubrie wrote to me and said: "My little brother, Calvin, is 9. Calvin plays football and swims and likes Lego and cars and bugs."*

Katie's Hair: *Katie's class in Joplin, Missouri, sent me a set of self-portraits.*

Page 13
Twins: *For Joanna, whose baby sisters were twins — age two.*

For Monique: *Monique wrote to me from Moose Jaw, Saskatchewan, and said that she loved to bug her stepbrother.*

Oh, Brother!: *To Diane from Saskatchewan who wrote me complaining about her brothers.*

Page 14
Chelsea's Dog Spot: *For Chelsea Mairs, Ballston Lake, New York. "I have a dog and we named him Spot. My dad does not like Spot."*

Lucy: *Donny wrote and told me about his dog named Lucy.*

Page 16
Jeanette Ran Red: *Jeanette sent me an e-mail wanting a spring poem.*

Page 18
Jayna's Shadow: *For Jayna, who sent an e-mail asking for a poem about shadows.*

Reading: *For Lora Wright in Arizona.*

Page 21
Goodnight: *For Andrew and Tyya Munsch, Guelph, Ontario.*

Scholastic Canada Ltd.
604 King Street West, Toronto, Ontario M5V 1E1, Canada

Scholastic Inc.
557 Broadway, New York, NY 10012, USA

Scholastic Australia Pty Limited
PO Box 579, Gosford, NSW 2250, Australia

Scholastic New Zealand Limited
Private Bag 94407, Botany, Manukau 2163, New Zealand

Scholastic Children's Books
Euston House, 24 Eversholt Street, London NW1 1DB, UK

Library and Archives Canada Cataloguing in Publication
Munsch, Robert N., 1945-
Neversink School and other silly poems / Robert Munsch ; illustrated by
Michael Martchenko. -- School market ed.

ISBN 978-1-4431-1335-9

I. Martchenko, Michael II. Title.

PS8576.U575N48 2011   jC811'.54   C2011-904396-3

LEGO ® is a trademark of The LEGO Group.

6 5 4 3 2 1   Printed in Canada 119   11 12 13 14